PUBLICITY POWER
A Practical Guide
To Effective Promotion

Charles Mallory

A FIFTY-MINUTE™ SERIES BOOK

CRISP PUBLICATIONS, INC.
Menlo Park, California

PUBLICITY POWER:
A Practical Guide to Effective Promotion

CREDITS
Editor: **Michael G. Crisp**
Designer: **Carol Harris**
Typesetting: **Interface Studio**
Cover Design: **Carol Harris**
Artwork: **Ralph Mapson**

All rights reserved. No part of this book may be reproduced or transmitted in any form or by any means now known or to be invented, electronic or mechanical, including photocopying, recording, or by any information storage or retrieval system without written permission from the author or publisher, except for the brief inclusion of quotations in a review.

Copyright © 1989 by Charles Mallory
Printed in the United States of America

English language Crisp books are distributed worldwide. Our major international distributors include:

CANADA: Reid Publishing Ltd., Box 69559—109 Thomas St., Oakville, Ontario, Canada L6J 7R4. TEL: (905) 842-4428, FAX: (905) 842-9327

Raincoast Books Distribution Ltd., 112 East 3rd Avenue, Vancouver, British Columbia, Canada V5T 1C8. TEL: (604) 873-6581, FAX: (604) 874-2711

AUSTRALIA: Career Builders, P.O. Box 1051, Springwood, Brisbane, Queensland, Australia 4127. TEL: 841-1061, FAX: 841-1580

NEW ZEALAND: Career Builders, P.O. Box 571, Manurewa, Auckland, New Zealand. TEL: 266-5276, FAX: 266-4152

JAPAN: Phoenix Associates Co., Mizuho Bldg. 2-12-2, Kami Osaki, Shinagawa-Ku, Tokyo 141, Japan. TEL: 3-443-7231, FAX: 3-443-7640

Selected Crisp titles are also available in other languages. Contact International Rights Manager Suzanne Kelly at (415) 323-6100 for more information.

Library of Congress Catalog Card Number 88-92737
Mallory, Charles
Publicity Power
ISBN 0-931961-82-3

This book is printed on recyclable paper with soy ink.

PREFACE

Public relations often remains an untapped resource for business today. Media publicity, a visible form of public relations, can bring financial gain and fame to any business, from a major corporation to Mom's Muffin Shoppe.

Advertising is expensive. A metro newspaper ad can cost $50 a column inch or more. Ads in trade magazines often cost in excess of $3,000 per page. Consumer magazines can easily be ten times higher. And broadcast advertising on prime time radio or television can be incredibly expensive!

Direct mail (the most cost-effective medium for many businesses) is not necessarily inexpensive. Direct mail costs include not only the development of the piece to be mailed (artwork, design, copywriting, etc.), but also the renting of lists, printing of letters and other materials, postage and handling, plus costs related to following-up the leads.

Regardless of the revenue that advertising or direct mail brings to a business, publicity can bring both revenue and recognition.

This book was developed for anyone wishing to know more about the power of publicity, including:

- business managers;
- small business owners and entrepreneurs;
- students in public relations courses;
- or those responsible for communications in nonprofit organizations.

In this book, you'll learn to write a query letter to a magazine, call a television producer, identify the most media-marketable aspect, and much more.

Happy promoting!

Charles Mallory

TO JOYCE

CONTENTS

INTRODUCTION 1

A BRIEF PUBLICITY GLOSSARY 3

PART ONE: DEVELOPING A PROMOTIONAL PLAN 7
    Building Your Plan 8
    Your Publicity Strategy 10
    Create Publicity Plan 13
    Sample Public Relations Plan #1 15
    Sample Public Relations Plan #2 16
    What Publicity Skills Do You Now Have? 18
    Publicity Ability Assessment 20
    What Publicity Work Requires 22
    Media Contacts 24

PART TWO: TAKING ACTION 27
    The Press Release 28
    The Press Release–Sample 31
    Create Your Own Press Release 33
    The Media Advisory 35
    Tips on Writing the Media Advisory 36
    Sample Media Advisory 37
    The Press Kit 38
    The Cover Letter 42
    Tips for Writing the Cover Letter 43
    Sample Cover Letter #1 44
    Sample Cover Letter #2 45
    The Fact Sheet 46
    Tips for Writing the Fact Sheet 46
    Sample Fact Sheet 47
    The Public Service Announcement 48
    Sample Public Service Announcements 49
    Press Kit Checklist 50
    Getting Magazine Placements 51
    Media Follow-Up Calls 52

PART THREE: THE OUTCOME 57
    You've Got An Interview! 58
    Radio Interview Tips 59
    TV Appearance Tips 60
    Getting More Mileage from Your Coverage Through Clips 61
    Ways to Use Clips 62
    Crisis Public Relations 63
    Holding An Event Checklist 65
    Summary 68

SUGGESTED READING 69

ABOUT THIS BOOK

PUBLICITY POWER is not like most books. It's more than a book to read; it's a book to use. The unique "self-paced" format of this book and the many worksheets encourage the reader to get involved and develop valuable approaches to gaining publicity.

PUBLICITY POWER can be used effectively in a number of ways. Here are some possibilities:

—**Self Study.** Because the book is self-instructional, all that is needed is a quiet place, and some time. By completing the activities and exercises, a reader should not only receive valuable feedback, but also practical ideas about how to develop a high-quality, effective promotional plan.

—**Workshops and Seminars.** The book is ideal for assigned reading prior to a workshop or seminar. With the basics in hand, the quality of the participation will improve, and more time can be spent on application during the program. The book is also effective when it is distributed at the beginning of a session, and participants "work through" the contents.

—**Remote Location Training.** Books can be sent to those not able to attend "home office" training sessions.

There are several other possibilities that depend on the objectives, program or ideas of the user. This book is ideal as a reference book and can be used again and again for various publicity needs.

INTRODUCTION

Publicity is a powerful tool for those who learn to use it effectively. To many, there is "magic" in being able to generate favorable publicity. This book will give you ideas about creating this magic. Like most other things, with a few basics and some practice, you can learn some of the secrets of generating "publicity power."

In Part I, you will learn how to establish a logical, workable publicity plan. Part II will provide methods for activating this plan and will cover publicity devices such as press releases, press kits, and radio announcements. Part III helps you prepare for interviews and appearances, and tells you how to plan special events.

After completing *Publicity Power*, you should have a solid understanding of how to generate favorable publicity for yourself and your organization without breaking the bank.

Good luck!

BECOME A NATURAL AT GENERATING POSITIVE PUBLICITY

PUBLICITY DEFINED

A simple definition of publicity is a method of disseminating information to attract public interest. Another, less accurate, but acceptable definition (for purposes served by this book), is "free advertising."

Public relations is simply telling people something favorable, such as what you do well. When you know how to approach it, you can get all the publicity you and your organization wants and deserves.

This book will show you how to maximize your return on the amount of time you invest. Publicity is not really "free" because it takes time. It does not, however, require a large cash outlay (unless, of course, you hire a major public relations firm to do your publicity for you). Learning how to create publicity effectively provides a genuine sense of accomplishment.

Publicity is not always easy to obtain. It takes practice, skill, enormous energy, endurance, and lots of time, but time can be your friend if you approach a project step-by-step.

Some people use the words "publicity" and "public relations" interchangeably. The glossary on the next page explains the differences among some of the words you have previously heard and will encounter several times in this book.

BRIEF GLOSSARY →

A BRIEF PUBLICITY GLOSSARY

ADVERTISING

Creating or changing attitudes, beliefs, and perceptions by influencing people with purchased broadcast time (radio, TV, audio or video-cassette) or print space (newspapers, magazines, journals, billboards) or other forms of written and/or visual media, (sky writing, leaflets, etc.).

EDITOR

A person responsible for the coordination, and/or the assessment of, a broadcast (including audio or video-cassettes) or printed feature. Assignment editors normally select story ideas; copy editors correct grammar and improve the quality of writing or flow of information; managing editors give direction to the overall effort.

MARKETING

A plan to inform an audience about a product or service so they will become customers. Marketing includes publicity, but also involves many other elements including research and development, pricing considerations, sales and sales training, distribution, packaging, and advertising.

MEDIA

Television, radio, newspapers, audio tapes, magazines, or a similar medium.

PLACEMENT

A broadcast interview or print-media article that was achieved via a public relations effort.

A BRIEF PUBLICITY GLOSSARY
(continued)

PRODUCER

The coordinator of a TV or radio news, talk or other show who is responsible for assembling stories and verifying the efforts of the necessary personnel to bring it to broadcast.

PROMOTION

Attracting attention to a product, service, or idea, through public relations or advertising.

PUBLIC RELATIONS

Creating or changing the attitudes, beliefs and perceptions of people by influencing them—primarily with information disseminated through the media.

PUBLICITY

A method of disseminating information that attracts public interest. Publicity can be provided in an almost unlimited number of ways, but it normally means coverage in television, radio, newspapers and/or magazines, and, as opposed to advertising, is often "free."

THERE ARE LOTS OF WAYS TO DISSEMINATE INFORMATION

PUBLIC RELATIONS VERSUS ADVERTISING

Many experts in public relations will tell you that P.R. (as it is commonly called), is better than advertising. Why? Because public relations carries weight; P.R. is often a third-party endorsement. When we see advertisements, we understand they are paid vehicles placed with the intention to sell us something. A favorable article in a newspaper or interview on radio or television, on the other hand, often appears to be information for the public. Studies have shown most people believe what the media tells them:

> "There's an 80 percent chance of rain today! Take your raincoat!"
>
> "The defendant knew about it all the time; I heard it on last night's news."
>
> "There was an article on them in the trade journal. Their business must really be doing well!"

Public relations pieces, carefully placed, are "ads" of a sort. Even with extensive P.R., an organization will normally also buy appropriate advertising because advertising can be controlled. The content, magnitude and timing of your message is controlled by you in advertising.

In public relations, an organization is at the mercy of others. You never know for sure how much print space you will get; how much time on the air you'll be allotted; or the outcome of an interview. You also don't always know the timing of the release. You do your best to take control of these elements to gain your desired outcome.

PART ONE

DEVELOPING A PROMOTIONAL PLAN

WHO
WHAT
WHY
WHERE
WHEN?

BUILDING YOUR PLAN

Think First

Building of a promotional plan begins with a careful examination of your objectives.

The first thing to determine is what you want to promote (i.e., a new product, a company reorganization, a public good deed, etc.). Decide carefully what you want publicity to do for your organization. If you want to sell products, don't emphasize non-relative items. Instead, focus on the benefits your products will provide.

Before you piece together a publicity plan, ask yourself the following questions:

1. Is The Time Right?
Has the product been announced or is it still in the testing stage? Will the message make more of an impact in six months or is now the best time for this promotional event?

There is no use promoting an item or issue if people can't relate to or react to it.

2. Is The Message Right?
Be careful how you promote. If you develop a flashy, memorable gimmick, you may be burdened with it for years. That's why you need to ensure your image is right.

Less-than-sparkling reputations follow companies that received bad publicity. Publicity sticks—for better or for worse, regardless of how things may have subsequently changed.

3. Are The Necessary Resources (Human or Monetary) Available?
To approach the media effectively, it is essential to have someone who can create high quality releases or letters and someone who is comfortable communicating with the media. Most people who are willing can learn these skills.

Determine where the publicity work will take place and assess what equipment you will need (i.e. postage machine, typewriter, personal computer, photocopier, etc.).

If you have special P.R. campaigns in mind, consider the finances and other requirements needed to carry out the task successfully.

BUILDING YOUR PLAN (continued)

More Considerations

The saying, "Plan your work and work your plan," is especially true for publicity. Careful planning allows for economical expenditure of time, money and energy. Through planning, you can focus your efforts for the results you want.

Ask yourself these questions to further develop a publicity plan:

1. Who is my target audience? (Does my topic suit the general public? Women? Pet owners? Psychologists?)

2. What are my resources? How much time and money are available?

3. What are my objectives? (Keep your target audience in mind and build your objectives to reach them. Considerably more information on this will be presented later in the book).

4. What are my strategies? (A television interview might be perfect; maybe a stunt in a hot-air balloon is better; perhaps only simple newspaper coverage is needed.)

YOUR PUBLICITY STRATEGY

Which media do you plan to use? Keep your goals in mind. If you want articles to help you generate sales locally on a revolutionary new product, you will need favorable newspaper and magazine articles, especially from the local media. If you want to promote your president as a professional speaker, a TV interview is right.

For many organizations, a "capabilities brochure," that explains the purposes of that organization, is a good idea. For other organizations, no such item is needed. These issues should be part of your publicity strategy.

You'll likely want several approaches to a P.R. campaign. Recognizing what you do best (perhaps you're better at writing than giving a workshop), may help you form your publicity strategy. As you think about your publicity plans, use the following checklist to plan which media you want and need.

For the campaign I have in mind, I want or need the following: (check those that apply)

BROCHURE

☐ Whole organization

☐ By topic:
  products,
  services,
  activities.

NEWSLETTER

☐ In-house (for staff members only)

☐ For clients

☐ For general public

YOUR PUBLICITY STRATEGY (continued)

TRADE SHOW/CONVENTION DISPLAY
- ☐ Local
- ☐ Regional
- ☐ National

PUBLIC APPEARANCES
- ☐ Local businesses
- ☐ Outlying businesses
- ☐ Trade show/convention

SEMINARS/WORKSHOPS
- ☐ For staff
- ☐ For clients
- ☐ For general public

DIRECT MAIL/TELEMARKETING
- ☐ Local target audience: _____.
- ☐ Regional target audience: _____.
- ☐ National target audience: _____.

MEDIA:

NEWSPAPERS
- ☐ Local/regional
    - ☐ News
    - ☐ Business
    - ☐ Entertainment
    - ☐ Other (fashion, food, home, sports, etc.)
    - ☐ Editorial page
- ☐ National

YOUR PUBLICITY STRATEGY
(continued)

MAGAZINES

☐ Local
    ☐ Business
    ☐ Other

☐ National trade, technical and professional
Subject Area: _____

☐ National consumer (newsstand and "popular" magazines)
Subject area: _____

RADIO

☐ Local
    ☐ News
    ☐ Talk shows

☐ National networks
    ☐ News
    ☐ Talk shows

TELEVISION

☐ Local
    ☐ Network affiliated
        ☐ News
        ☐ Talk shows
    ☐ Cable
        ☐ News (if existent)
        ☐ Talk shows

☐ National
    ☐ Networks
        ☐ News
        ☐ Talk/entertainment shows
    ☐ Cable
        ☐ News
        ☐ Talk shows

HOW NOT TO DEVELOP A PUBLICITY STRATEGY!

CREATE A PUBLICITY PLAN

ORGANIZATION:

Define your organization (small business, non-profit association, entrepreneurial venture, subsidiary, etc.). Include a brief description of your organization's unique features, as well as your basic products or services.

LIST YOUR MARKETING OBJECTIVES:

What product or service am I attempting to promote? In some organizations, promotion might be a fundraising effort or a goal related to human values.

LIST YOUR PUBLIC RELATIONS OBJECTIVES:

In what ways do you want to shape public opinion? (If your answer does not relate to the marketing objective you listed above; re-think your public relations objectives.)

DESCRIBE WHERE THINGS STAND NOW (in publicity exposure):

Include all related printed articles, broadcast appearances, brochures, and other forms of information relating to your public relations objectives.

DESCRIBE THE OUTCOME YOU DESIRE:

Name your hoped-for coverage in newspapers, magazines, radio, TV; being invited to selected functions; being asked to serve on a special committee, etc. Think carefully about which coverage will help you best achieve your objectives.

CREATE A PUBLICITY PLAN
(continued)

DESCRIBE YOUR TARGET AUDIENCE:

To whom do you want to sell products or services, or reach with your message? "Everybody" is not the answer. Think carefully about your objectives and focus your efforts toward those who will be attracted to your message.

DEFINE THE TARGET MEDIA YOU PLAN TO USE:

First review your "target audience" and then re-read "Where I want to be." Calculate which publicity efforts will reach the key people you wish to influence.

DEVELOP YOUR STRATEGIES:

List specific steps and how you will carry them out. Name those responsible for writing press releases, calling the media, developing the flyer, organizing the event, etc. You should also develop a rough timetable for the completion of each step.

SAMPLE P.R. PLANS AHEAD →

SAMPLE PUBLIC RELATIONS PLAN #1

Organization: Emily Stevens, Professional Speaker

Specialty: Speech to large audiences about how technology and society can work more productively together.

Marketing objectives: To raise speaking fee from $500 to $1,000 by end of next year; to increase incoming requests for speeches by 25% by end of year.

Public relations objectives: To gain exposure through media that demonstrates public speaking skills and knowledge of technology in society; to be viewed as a professional speaker who is ''in demand.''

Where things now stand: Included in one article in suburban newspaper, under ''New Business'' column.

The desired outcome: The most publicized new professional speaker in the field of technology by the end of this year. National recognition by end of the following year.

Target audience: Meeting planners and human resource development directors (primary); general public (secondary).

Target media:

- Local TV-network affiliated stations;
- Local radio, ''*The Henry Fowler Show*;''
- Local newspapers in this region: (preferably full-length feature stories);
- Feature article in *Corporate* Magazine.

Strategies: Develop press kit with photos. Send to target media and follow up with calls. Get involved with ''Technology in Society Foundation,'' both in fundraising and in giving no-fee speeches.

Second strategy: (if needed): Work with local high-tech companies on developing ''Technology Awareness Day.'' Get on program with nationally recognized celebrity speaker. When event coordinated, prepare news release and send to all target media; follow up with calls.

SAMPLE PUBLIC RELATIONS PLAN #2

Organization: Topline Computer Center (single store that sells computer-related products)

Marketing Objectives:

- Attract new customers to store.
- Gain repeat business from previous customers.

Promotional Objectives:

- Increase community awareness of the store.
- Position store as a friendly, helpful computer resource, especially for those new to computing.
- Establish perception of store as a good community citizen.

Strategies:

- Store owner to give speeches to local groups.

GROUP	TOPIC
Parent/Teacher organization	The Value of Computers in Education
Civic Clubs	Computers and the Future
Small Business Association	How a Microcomputer Can Help Your Business
Writers' Club	Word Processing: An Invaluable Tool
Center City Art Designers Association	Desktop Publishing: The Future Is Here

PLAN #2 (continued)

- "Coffee and Computers with Dan and Bob." Once-a-month free coffee, tea, and pastries, at 7:00 a.m. store opening. Local radio station invited to premier event. Purpose: to demonstrate and answer questions about personal computers to non-owners. Sales managers Dan and Bob will host the event.

- Topline Scholars Program. Provide a scholarship for a deserving student intending to major in computer science. The media will be informed when the scholarship is announced and awarded.

- Write press release to feature John, Topline's 17-year-old salesperson. Focus on John being admitted to college at age 16, plus his expertise in advanced programming.

- Sponsor booth at upcoming Personal Computer Trade Show in Center City. Provide small cakes in the shape of personal computers to those stopping by booth.

- Initiate a "Computer Counselor" column in *Center City News*. Have John and Dan write material which will answer the general public's questions about computers.

WHAT PUBLICITY SKILLS DO YOU NOW HAVE?

Take the following quiz to find out your level of ability to generate publicity. Don't be dismayed if your score is lower than you expected. This survey will identify areas that need improvement.

PUBLICITY-ABILITY ASSESSMENT

For the items listed below, rate your ability from 1 to 5 by circling the appropriate number.

- 5 = Very comfortable.
- 4 = Moderately comfortable.
- 3 = Somewhat comfortable.
- 2 = Uncomfortable.
- 1 = Fearful/very uncomfortable.

	LOW				HIGH
1. Talking about the organization or event to be promoted—to friends or family.	1	2	3	4	5
2. Convincing others why they should be interested in something of interest to you (not necessarily the item to be promoted).	1	2	3	4	5
3. Articulating an idea that might be foreign to the listener.	1	2	3	4	5
4. Writing a letter to an editor or producer suggesting a story idea.	1	2	3	4	5
5. Following up a letter with a phone call to an editor or producer to verbally suggest an idea.	1	2	3	4	5

PUBLICITY SKILLS (continued)

		LOW				HIGH
6.	Responding on the phone to an editor who says impatiently: "What are you promoting?"	1	2	3	4	5
7.	Being introduced to a recognized media personality who asks you about yourself.	1	2	3	4	5
8.	Making 20 "cold calls" to discuss a story idea.	1	2	3	4	5
9.	Re-working a story idea that has been rejected by every editor and producer to whom it was sent.	1	2	3	4	5
10.	Planning a mailing, completing a follow-up phone campaign, scheduling an event and ensuring all details handled.	1	2	3	4	5

> There are no right or wrong answers. All situations are similar to those required to obtain publicity. See the next page an analysis of your scoring.

PUBLICITY ABILITY ASSESSMENT

Following are some guidelines to measure your skills.

COMFORTABLE WITH...	BUT NOT...	COMMENT
1	2,3,5,6,8	Work on feeling comfortable about discussing idea with strangers.*
2,3,5,6,8	4	You'll do great with the phone work, but might need some writing assistance.**
8,9	–	You show great persistence. This is a wonderful skill for public relations professionals.
2,3,5	8,9	You have the required verbal skills; your endurance skills seem to need some work.

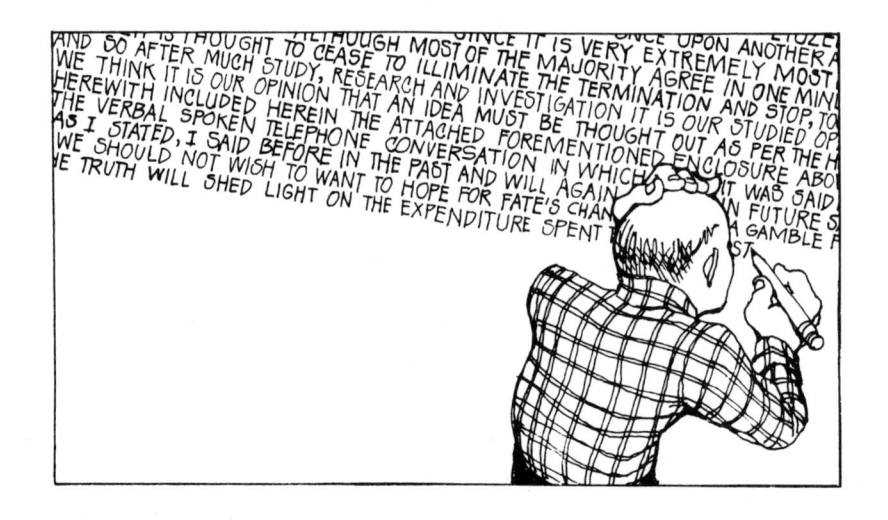

PUBLICITY ABILITY ASSESSMENT (continued)

COMFORTABLE WITH...	BUT NOT...	COMMENT
7	–	Some apprehension is normal, but stay friendly and prepare thoughtful questions for the media.
–	10	You appear to need help on organization, which is a must for successful public relations planning.
–	6	You're normal. Even seasoned professionals can be uncomfortable when confronted, but they pursue it anyway.

*A handy guide for you might be *Developing Positive Assertiveness*.

**For a good manual on developing writing skills, order *Better Business Writing* from the back of this book.

WHAT PUBLICITY WORK REQUIRES

The following key factors are required for successful publicity results. Remember, skills can be learned! If you have the following talents and abilities, capitalize on them. If you don't, start developing them.

1. PERSONAL ENERGY

Enthusiasm is always useful, but especially in generating publicity. It is your bulwark when time pressures mount or things are not developing as planned. Often *persistence* gets the job done. There is no substitute for sticking with a project.

2. WRITING ABILITY

Successful publicity requires good writing. If you write well, you are well on your way to success. If you need help, get it by enrolling in a writing class or reading a book like *Writing Fitness* which may be ordered using the form in the back of this book.

3. VERBAL ABILITY

The best verbal approach for media publicity is a person who can relate ideas clearly, listen to the response, and quickly adapt the message to be of interest to the media party. If your verbal skills need work, enroll in a speech class or buy a self-study book such as *The Art of Communication* or *Influencing Others*, either of which can be ordered using the information in the back of this book.

WHAT PUBLICITY REQUIRES
(continued)

4. ORGANIZATION

A full publicity plan includes a myriad of details. A well-organized person will save time and energy. Major publicity campaigns can seem overwhelming. There can be dozens of letters to write, numerous follow-up calls to make, press releases to prepare, events to schedule, etc.. This is why planning tools such as checklists and computerized data bases can be invaluable.

*"WE NEED THE POSTER BY SUNDOWN.
THE PUBLICITY DIRECTOR HAS SPOKEN."*

MEDIA CONTACTS

Some people maintain that the key to public relations is "contacts—knowing the right people." It is helpful, but not essential. Approaching the media in a professional manner is the real key. Part of that involves knowing who to approach and how.

If your publicity plans call for a regional or national campaign, you'll need a directory of media. There are several available and any reference librarian will be able to show them to you. One that is easy to use and read is a Bacon's media directory. Each media listing in a Bacon's directory includes names, address, and phone numbers. It is possible to order labels for most media individuals you wish to contact (i.e., all U.S. weekly newspapers, etc.). The directories are coil-bound and lay flat for ease of reference use.

For United States listings:

Radio and Television Listings
Bacon's Radio/TV Directory
322 S. Michigan Avenue
Chicago, IL 60604
1-800-621-0561
(Contains all radio and TV listings in the U.S.)

Newspaper and Magazine Listings
Bacon's Publicity Checker
322 S. Michigan Avenue
Chicago, IL 60604
1-800-621-0561
(Contains U.S. and Canadian listings; two volumes)

For other countries:

Newspaper and Magazine Listings
Bacon's International Publicity Checker
(One volume; includes 12,000 magazines and 1,000 national and regional newspapers in 15 Western European countries, including the United Kingdom)

In most situations, a good listing of local media is all you will need. It is wise to compile your own list and update it as needed. This is when a computer data base becomes very worthwhile. If you're in a large city, you can often buy a copy of a local media list that has been compiled by a public relations firm.

COMPILE YOUR OWN MEDIA LIST

To compile your own list, use a computer data base if possible. Otherwise, use a flexible format (such as a three-ring binder) and call each media outlet to get the basic information. You should update your directory every six months. In the interim, make personnel changes when you discover them.

Following are suggested ways to format your media directory:

Newspaper Sample Listing

Name:

Frequency: Daily _____   Weekly _____   Other: _____

Mailing Address:

Street Address:

Managing Editor*:

Business Editor:

Assignment Editor**:

Community Affairs Editor:

(Specialty) Editor***:

Photo Editor:

Deadlines:

---

*The Managing Editor is usually the highest level of hands-on editor; don't mail items to the Executive Editor, Editorial Editor or Editor-in-Chief; if there is no Managing Editor, look for Editor.

**Some newspapers have an Assignment Editor, can decide what's worth writing about and what isn't.

***If your business falls into a category where you need to contact a specific section or topic editor (Real Estate, Fashion, Food, Automotive, Gardening, Education, etc.) list it here. If the newspaper doesn't have an editor for your particular field, use the name of the other editors listed above. Don't try to send something to "Fun and Fitness Editor," and hope the staff will be amused.

NOTE: This page may be copied or adapted without further permission.

COMPILE YOUR OWN MEDIA LIST
(continued)

Radio/TV Sample Listing

Radio/TV Station (call letters):

Number on dial: _____ AM _____ FM or _____ channel

Mailing Address:

Street Address:

News Director:

Assignment Editor:

Programs of Interest*:

1. _____

   Producer:

   Host:

   Airing time and Length:

   Lead time needed**:

   Live or Taped?:

   Format***:

2. (etc.)

---

*Listen to the station and find out which programs could be suitable for you. Don't include the news; if something is news, just mail the item to the News Director.

**"Lead time" refers to how far ahead the producer books guests for the show. It might be as little as a week or as much as 2-3 months. Don't try to bend the lead time rules.

***What is the format of the show? Are there three guests at once, addressing a single topic? Does one guest get a whole hour? Are there call-ins? These details will be important, should you get scheduled to appear.

NOTE: This page may be copied or adapted without further permission.

PART TWO

TAKING ACTION

THE PRESS RELEASE

The press release is the primary tool of public relations. A well-done press release is essentially a brief article designed to stimulate media coverage. Great care needs to be taken while developing your press release. Later in this section you will have an opportunity to create one based on some sound principles. Regardless of how good your final effort is, do not assume that your press release will be printed verbatim, although this has been known to happen.

Media people have varying opinions about press releases. Any recipient will know that it is not necessarily news because it probably contains some plumped-up copy designed to make something particularly appealing. It doesn't matter if your stationery has "News Release" at the top, or a similar phrase, it is still a press release.

Some people disregard press releases because they consider them the same as an advertisement. Others view press releases as sources of information or idea-generators.

Some press releases have more value than others to the media. This book will teach you to create one that will get more attention for your message.

THE PRESS RELEASE (continued)

Three good ways to make your press releases stand out are:

1. Don't send too many.

2. Write them, or have them written, as closely as possible to the style of a news story. Make sure they answer the following five basics: Who? What? When? Where? Why? plus, when appropriate, How?

3. Present them cleanly and clearly, double-spaced on non-fancy stationery or paper, with the typing perfect and the letters easily readable.

When writing your release, make sure you know the answers to the five basics plus one. Then determine which to include. For instance, if the reason your event is being held is to gain publicity, it would not be a good idea to include that item in your press release!

THE PRESS RELEASE (continued)

Journalism students are taught the "inverted pyramid." This is an excellent structure to use for a press release, since it is an ideal way to tell a story. When developing your next press release, try using the inverted pyramid style presented below:

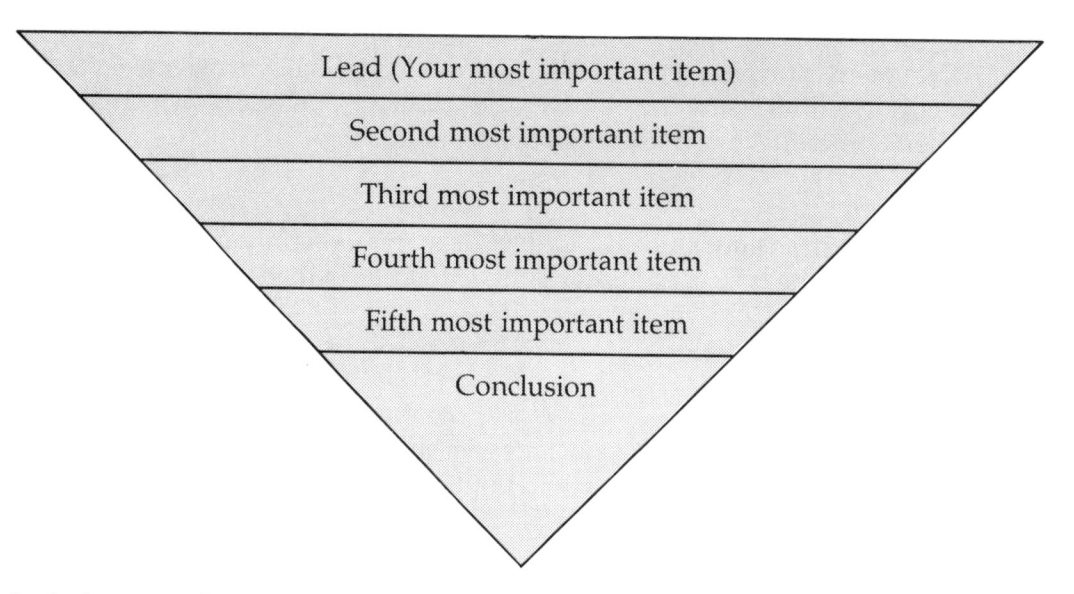

```
Lead (Your most important item)
Second most important item
Third most important item
Fourth most important item
Fifth most important item
Conclusion
```

Include as much relevant information as you like, but keep your release to one or two pages.

A *lead* should start your story with a nugget that summarizes the point of your release. This is not the place to include lots of details, give long quotes, or relate complex information.

It might seem logical to "build up" to more important aspects as magazine feature articles often do, but it is better to follow a "newspaper" example and "cut from the bottom" to keep your release brief and powerful. A good press release will allow a reader to rapidly glance through the information to assess if the story is of interest.

Following is a sample press release. Although this example may be longer and more ambitious than ones you will be writing, it points out various components that are important to a press release.

SAMPLE PRESS RELEASE

The Press Release

Don't send the release until you're ready to talk about the subject; then use this.

Give editors an easy way to reach you or your public relations representatives.

Contact Twyla Dell at
555-2514 (office) or
555-2454 (home)

FOR IMMEDIATE RELEASE:

Start out strong, but legitimate.

'AN HONEST DAY'S WORK' ENCOURAGES PRODUCTIVITY

Simple, clean; this can be more creative, if necessary. Don't get too long or too gimmicky.

The message is simple yet seems difficult for most businesses to learn: give employees what they want, and they'll give employers what they want. Author Twyla Dell asserts this belief to managers in seminars, consulting, and through her new book, *An Honest Day's Work: Motivating Employees to Give Their Best* (Crisp Publications, Menlo Park, California, 1988).

A splash of biography.

A management trainer for the past few years, Dell has made this message the focus of her company, Twyla Dell Presents. Though the days of "crack the whip" bosses seem long gone, many such supervisors are still around. Other managers simply do not understand how to get workers to give their best. Dell's book helps managers close the "Commitment Gap," stop "Time Theft," and increase employee effectiveness.

Colorful language helps propel story.

A subtle additional mention of product (book).

"The best way to develop motivated committed employees is both easy and free," says Dell. "Give employees what they want: Interesting work, recognition, respect, challenge, and opportunities for skill development. Listen to them, inform them, let them see the end result of their work–and give them credit for a job when it is done well. If you do this, employees will give you what you want: loyalty, enthusiasm and productivity."

Make quotes sound smooth.

This fuller background comes in late; don't push it too close to the beginning of the story.

Twyla Dell has worked in public schools, private industry and government. She taught high school English and Spanish for 12 years, and then returned to school for a Master's degree in English.

more

SAMPLE PRESS RELEASE (continued)

Don't be shy of mentioning other businesses; specificity helps.

2.

These facts give the product (book) extra authority.

Dell then worked for the Environmental Protection Agency and developed training materials for Western Auto's managers and store owners. Since 1985, she has been president of Twyla Dell Presents, a consulting firm specializing in productivity.

In her book, *An Honest Day's Work,* Dell relates several case histories of managers who solved problems by recognizing the needs of staff members. Dell interviewed a number of managers and executives while researching material for her book. Self-assessment steps from these interviews are summarized to help managers create higher levels of productivity.

Quotes that lead to visualization are a plus.

The agenda for business in the next several years, says Dell, is to create a workplace that will grow people *and* profits. "We're moving from a task-centered workplace, where output and capital equipment are the most important assets, to a person-centered workplace in which employees become the most important assets. The greatest demand in the future will be for workers who know how to grow and adapt to a changing economy."

Catchy name adds extra interest, keeps story moving.

Positioning the author as a futurist gives added impact.

The least important part; that's why it's at the end.

Managers who know how to develop their people, liberate their talents, and get the best from them have always been highly prized. Such managers are "Great People Motivators" and Dell tells "How to Become a Great People Motivator" in her program based on her research, interviews and book.

A nice conclusion gives the release the seal of professionalism, even though the editor usually cuts from the bottom upward when editing the story.

Developing the skills of managers to become "the boss for whom others love to work," is not just a nice idea, according to Dell. "It's an investment for increased productivity and better service." As she says in her book, "Service is given to people by people. To give excellent service, it is essential that people feel good about themselves and their job."

#

A standard end mark.

CREATE YOUR OWN PRESS RELEASE

Think about a situation where you want to create some positive publicity for your organization—then answer the questions on the worksheet below:

1. The purpose of your release?

2. The main point of your release? (this will become your lead:)

3. The elements:

    Who?

    What?

    When?

    Where?

    Why?

    How?

4. Which elements to include in the press release:

	Yes	No
Who?	___	___
What?	___	___
When?	___	___
Where?	___	___
Why?	___	___
How?	___	___

If you've checked "no" for most items you may have a problem. Re-think your concept and develop a media approach that is newsworthy.

NOTE: This form may be copied without further permission from the publisher.

WRITING YOUR RELEASE

Begin writing the release based on the information outlined. You don't have to write it out completely unless that is easiest for you. Perhaps it's easier for you to write everything before you write a lead and conclusion. This would allow you to write several versions before selecting the best one.

Keep your copy as objective as possible. Phrases such as, "the best service around," or "a very popular place," do not belong. Instead, concentrate on assessments: "The leading manufacturer of," "one of the top five companies for" (if it truly seems to be a leader), "named the best in customer service by the association for..." and the like. Remember, you are not writing an advertisement.

Leave out items you don't want to promote. Don't include negative information. Make sure your information is accurate. If you can't verify it, don't include it. Grammar and spelling must be perfect. If you aren't certain about your skills in this area, work with someone who will ensure these items are professionally handled.

Write a succinct straightforward headline and type "For Immediate Release" at the top (unless it doesn't apply for some reason).

THE PRESS RELEASE HAS BEEN AROUND A LONG TIME

THE MEDIA ADVISORY

A media advisory is a valuable tool if you're having a high-visibility event that can be covered by local TV media. While you hope to gain coverage from newspapers and radio as well, this visual-oriented method works best for cultivating TV coverage.

Careful planning is always required to promote the value of your concept. It is never a good idea, however, to put all your hopes into broadcast media coverage, for if a big news day occurs (such as a local tragedy), your event might not ever make it on the air.

Your main goal in holding an event is to gain media attendance. However, some other value should be worked into your event, in case the media decides not to show up. Media advisories work to announce an event only if they are used sparingly. You won't receive once-a-month coverage from the local TV station just because you send a media advisory every month. Producers and editors are wary of giving too much exposure to one organization, cause, or person—unless the subject has unusual interest or is highly controversial.

Media advisories are normally the domain of large organizations. Do not assume, however, that being big is a necessary prerequisite to receive news coverage. TV producers are interested in visual, fast-moving, interesting personalities, and captivating stories. If such a story comes from your business, you can receive substantial coverage.

TIPS ON WRITING THE MEDIA ADVISORY

1. Most importantly: only issue a media advisory if you reasonably expect media to attend. It must be related to a specific newsworthy announcement or event. A media advisory should never be used to announce a sale, or communicate something that normally occurs.

2. Determine the viability of sending a media advisory for an event by objectively evaluating whether your idea has a strong visual factor that would be good for TV media. For example, instead of your organization merely giving money to instruct kids about fire safety, you might convince a local fire station to have an open house, complete with polished fire trucks, balloons, Dalmatians, and safety coloring books sponsored by your organization. This kind of visual angle will be more likely to attract TV media.

   To gain outside perspective on an event that might attract media, query others on their interest level of your event before you plan and schedule it.

3. Keep your media advisory short and to the point. Don't trump it up. List the subject of the media advisory (in plain language), time, place, and the contact person's name and phone number. In a few paragraphs, list some details to flesh out the story. A length of one page is best.

4. Sending out a media advisory is not the same as calling a press conference. You're simply inviting the media to attend an event. In the truest sense, you are hosting the event and asking the media if they would be interested in attending. At no point should you announce your event as being "for" the media.

SAMPLE MEDIA ADVISORY

MEDIA ADVISORY

Subject: Skip Jones Gives Skateboard Demonstration

Time: 12:30 p.m., Saturday, September 23

Place: Shinnick Skateboards, 6625 Jefferson, Center City, Missouri

Contact: Martin Elliott, 555-3290

Skip Jones, the teen-age "king of the skateboarders," will make an appearance at 12:30 p.m., Thursday. Known for his daring stunts, Skip will give a demonstration of new skateboarding techniques, which he says are "more spectacular and safer than I used to win last year's national championship."

Skip Jones recently became the national spokesperson for Zyfly Skateboards. During his appearance at the Shinnick store, he will unveil the new line of Zyfly Dashers, which have been described as "skateboards of the future."

An interview with Skip Jones or with James Shinnick, president of Shinnick Skateboards, can be arranged by calling Martin Elliott at 555-3290.

THE PRESS KIT

A press release is an item to mail or provide to the press. A press kit is used to give the media an array of informational pieces.

Many businesses have a packet of information that they provide to customers. These normally include brochures, coupons, photographs, company newsletters, or other items. These are intended to give information which will help explain a business and its goals.

A press kit is similar, except that the recipients are the media. They need clear, concise information about the organization to have sufficient information, should they decide to write about the company.

There is no predetermined set of items that a press kit must include. Here are three ways a press kit may be assembled:

1	2	3
1. Press release 2. Bio 3. Fact sheet	1. Cover letter 2. Press release 3. Bio 4. Photos 5. Fact sheet 6. Pre-written interview or sample questions.	1. Press release 2. Bio 3. Fact Sheet 4. PSAs.

Do you always need a press kit to approach the media? No. If you simply send a release to mention something new or to announce an event, it will normally be sufficient. The media will call you if they don't have enough information. A press kit is useful for promoting an organization on a broad basis. It supports a publicity campaign that is ongoing.

THE PRESS KIT (continued)

PRE-WRITTEN INTERVIEW

A pre-written interview is just that. It contains questions and answers that are fully developed and written out. Pre-written interviews are effective. A reporter or editor can re-write the information into a story with quotes, or simply use it as background information.

SAMPLE QUESTIONS

Some press kits contain a brief list of questions about the item being promoted. If you create "sample questions" take care to balance them. You want them to be used in such a way they present your point. However, if they are too slanted or commercial ("What's the price of the new software package and where is it available?"), you establish an immediate lack of credibility and your questions are unlikely to be used.

BIOGRAPHY

In many instances, a bio will be important for your promotion. Keep "bios" crisp and unadorned. Include the basics: education, occupation, (prior occupations if pertinent), awards and honors. Mention spouse and children near the end, unless the family is important to the promotional campaign (such as a family-owned business).

Which bios should be included in a press kit? Typically, the larger the organization, the more will be included. Normally bios should be kept to a minimum. More than three bios begin to melt into one less-interesting group. Determine which people truly need to be featured.

For a press kit featuring one person (a consultant, professional speaker, a performer, and the like), a bio is a must, not an option.

THE PRESS KIT (continued)

PHOTOS

If photographs are to be included in the press kit, it is best to send black-and-white glossy 8" X 10" or 5" X 7" photos. Determine your true needs with photographs. It is nice to have a photo follow a bio. Sometimes a press kit can be enhanced by an action shot of people doing something relevent. For a product or well-known personality, photos are a necessity. If a procedure, product or service is difficult to describe in writing, sometimes a photo can do the work for you. Do not send a photo of a building (i.e. a company headquarters) unless the building is essential to the story.

If color is an absolute must for your press kit, include a transparency or slide. Color is a "must" for magazines that might use a color shot, or when the product or service would be unfairly portrayed if only a black-and-white was provided.

Don't send snapshots or casual photos. If you cannot afford or do not know a professional photographer, it is better to have no photos than to include an unprofessional one.

Caption your photos either by typing information on a label and applying it to the back of the photo or typing the info on a sheet of paper and taping the top of the sheet to the back of the photo.

CLIENT LIST/REFERRAL LETTERS

Some press kits include client lists. For instance, a small laboratory that does work for internationally known companies would benefit by showing a client list. It is essential that the client's permission be obtained.

Referral letters can also be useful, especially if they are from well-known people or companies. Such letters can support what is proclaimed in the press release. Referral letters are not needed for most press kits because normally the media will not use a referral letter in an article or interview.

THE PRESS KIT (continued)

CLIPS

A "clip" in a press kit is a copy of a previously published article. For more information on how to use clips effectively, see the "Getting More Mileage out of Your Coverage" on page 61.

ADDITIONAL ITEMS

Don't feel that you need to re-invent the press kit (adding a catalog, advertisement, or other unconventional inclusion) to gain attention. Those who make use of press kits will pay attention to solid facts and an interesting story. They are seldom interested in self-serving advertising.

THE PACKAGE

The "package" is a folder that contains all the pieces that make up the press kit.

Flashy packages for media kits often will work against you. Bright orange color or gigantic letters might make the package "stand out" on an editor's desk, but you might sacrifice your credibility. If sales-oriented copy is printed on the package, an editor or reporter might give the press kit even less consideration.

A quiet dignified folder with inside pockets will suffice for most press kits. Choose a conservative or bright color, but nothing outlandish. One option is to apply a typed label on the cover with the name of the individual or organization to be promoted. Your cover letter will normally be paper-clipped to the folder.

THE COVER LETTER

When a press kit is received, the person receiving it realizes it is filled with several sheets of information. Usually they quickly assess it for usefulness or interest.

A sloppy package will tell the recipient that the approach isn't professional. The materials inside thereby get half a chance. Extremely hard-to-read type is another strike against a press kit.

Even if the package is sharp and the type clean, a long, rambling cover letter tells an editor: "Don't look inside. There's more of this."

Cover letters should be on letterhead. If letterhead isn't available, a neatly-typed letter that contains an address and phone number will do the trick.

Open your cover letter with a positive, brief statement. Invite the reader to refer to the press kit. Make sure your name and address are clearly visible on the cover letter. Then let your press kit do the work.

TIPS FOR WRITING THE COVER LETTER

1. Think of the most interesting aspect of what you're promoting. Choose vivid aspects over general ones to start your letter. Cover the subject in two or three sentences.

2. Though you are making a sales pitch, avoid a hard push. Never say, "You'll want to cover this story," or "This would make an excellent TV report." Describe what you're promoting in an enthusiastic and inviting way.

3. Follow your introductory paragraph with a mention of the press kit or press release attached.

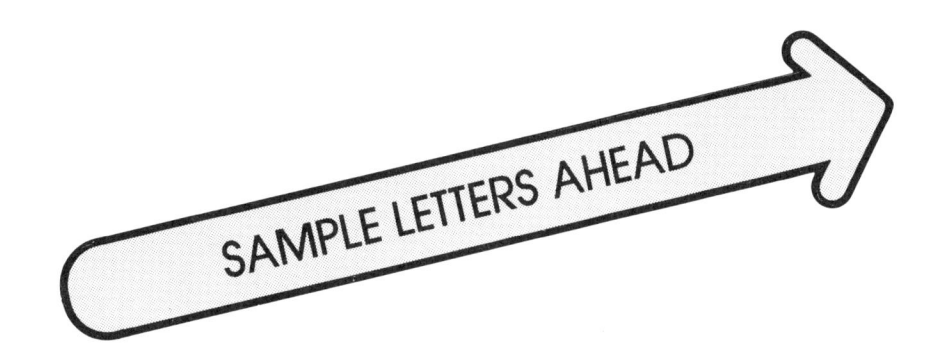

SAMPLE LETTERS AHEAD →

SAMPLE COVER LETTER —1

N-HOME INSURANCE
233 Osgood Street
Shawnee Mission, KS 66201

October 12, 19xx

John Doe
Producer, 61 News
KJLM-TV
Shawnee Mission, KS 66201

Dear Mr. Doe:

Life insurance, homeowners insurance, car insurance—they have been around so long we're used to them.

Now, due to rising health care costs, a new form has emerged–nursing home insurance. Families find they can't afford to place aging parents in a nursing home for fear of going broke. Costs of $1,000 a week are not futuristic fiction. They're a reality!

The enclosed information will tell you more about this crucial, timely issue. I would be happy to help you develop a story about nursing home insurance and how families are beginning to view this form of insurance as essential.

Sincerely,

Matilda Burton Fowler

N-Home Insurance
233 Osgood Street
Shawnee Mission, KS 66201

SAMPLE COVER LETTER #2

BLAINE FARM SUPPLY
9700 W. 72nd Street
Blaine, Ohio 45678

October 12, 19xx

Melvin Doe
Editor
Cleveland County Monitor
Blaine, OH 45678

Dear Mr. Doe:

Perhaps the most startling crime in our community's history happened on a sunny Sunday morning in 1876 during church services at the Blaine Church of the Rising Sun. During hymns, three bandits entered the church and began robbing people. The history-making twist to the story is how the minister quietly talked the robbers into giving up a life of crime.

To mark the 150th anniversary of this event, Blaine Farm Supply (which is located on the former site of the Blaine Church of the Rising Sun) is sponsoring a play, "Temptation to Topple a Temple." The play will be presented in December at the Blaine High School.

The leading character, Rev. Farrell Divers, will be played by Scott Johnson, a high school senior. who plans to major in theatre at the University of Ohio. Two of the playwrights, employees at Blaine Farm Supply, are avid researchers of the town's history.

Enclosed is a press release with more information. Thank you for considering this story idea.

Sincerely,

George Botkins

9700 W. 72nd Street
Blaine, OH 45678

THE FACT SHEET

A fact sheet is a handy way to give basic information on an organization. It does not replace a press release in making an announcement, nor is it connected to a specific event. While it might seem like dry reading, it gives important facts. The length can vary, but two, double-spaced, typewritten pages or less is a good length.

Tips On Writing A Fact Sheet

1. List the address of the organization at the top. Then list basic information under headings: founded (when and by whom), number of employees, and work performed (products produced, sold, distributed, etc., or services provided). You can also list such things as annual sales, etc., if this not private information.

2. Follow with a brief history of the organization. Mention major changes in products/services provided, or a shift in key players. This is not the place for anecdotes. This also is not the place for "puffery" or to push a specific promotion. For an event or an item requiring immediacy, use a press release. The fact sheet should be usable for a lengthy period of time without requiring change.

SAMPLE FACT SHEET

Jane Walters
555-6446

FACT SHEET

Gregg Novelties, Inc.

622 W. Overland Street, Center City, Missouri 66009

Founded: 1959, by Joseph Gregg, in Topeka, Kansas

Number of Employees: 31

Product Lines: Sunglasses, games, costumes, gag gifts

Brief History:

Gregg Novelties, Inc., originally called Gregg Importers, was founded in 1959 by Joseph Gregg in Topeka, Kansas. Gregg imported clothing and accessories for a variety of stores throughout the Midwest.

In the early 1960s, the firm de-emphasized and ultimately discontinued clothing sales and focused on accessories. It was considered the leader in the Midwest for imported jewelry, scarves, and hats. In 1969, the company acquired CircusZack Novelties, and gradually shifted its business to supplying novelty items to gift stores and theatres. Joseph Gregg, Jr., son of the founder, became president of the company in 1975. Joseph Gregg, Sr., continues to serve as chairman of the board.

Perhaps the most well-known item sold by the company is the Gregg Yo-Yo, which has been touted by yo-yo champions and is considered a quality product by yo-yo aficionados.

#

THE PUBLIC SERVICE ANNOUNCEMENT

A public service announcement is a short piece (usually 10 or 30 seconds) written in script form for radio or TV use. It is much more likely to be used on radio than TV. It is normally impossible to place unless used for a nonprofit organization, or is related to an event held for a nonprofit organization or cause. The "PSA," as it is called, should be sent to radio and TV stations in the vicinity of your organization. Some PSAs are tied to a specific event. Others, designed to merely promote awareness, are used anytime.

At the top of a PSA is a "kill date," or date to stop using the piece. For an announcement that may not have a time limit, you can list "none" or list a date two months away (just to stimulate its use within that time span.) Though PSAs can be written in a variety of lengths, 10-second and 30-second versions are most common. Try sending two versions of a PSA—a 10-second version and a 30-second version. Don't send more than two amounts at once. Also, don't bombard radio and TV stations with too many PSAs. If a specific day, week, or month ties to your organization (World Peace Day, National Diabetes Month, etc.) you should send extra PSA material. The connection to a specific point in time increases the likelihood of your PSA being used.

Tips On Writing Your Public Service Announcements

1. Make the language easily readable. Read it to yourself several times. Don't cram in extra information. Make it easy for the recipient by giving your PSA the proper length.

2. Keep the message in a 10-second release very simple. One sentence is probably sufficient to make your statement. It is a good idea to give a phone number or other contact/date information.

3. PSAs are more likely to be used if they are tied to a specific event or related to a good cause. They are not a substitute for an advertisement.

SAMPLE PUBLIC SERVICE ANNOUNCEMENT

SAMPLE 10-SECOND PUBLIC SERVICE ANNOUNCEMENT:

Regina Schwartz
555-6421

:10   BUDDIES OF THE ZOO

KILL DATE: September 20, 19xx

ANNCR: MAKE A FRIEND WHO'S A REAL ANIMAL! BECOME A 'BUDDY OF THE ZOO' WITH CENTER CITY ZOO. CALL 5-5-5, 1-7-3-3 FOR MORE INFORMATION.

SAMPLE 30-SECOND PUBLIC SERVICE ANNOUNCEMENT

Bruce Nouline
555-6421

:30   MUFFINS MEAN HUGS

KILL DATE: November 15, 19xx

ANNCR: MUFFINS-MEAN-HUGS, FOR THE STOP CHILD-ABUSE ASSOCIATION. ALL PROCEEDS FROM MUFFINS SOLD THIS WEEK AT MOM'S MUFFINS, AT SIX LOCATIONS IN CENTER CITY, WILL GO TO THE STOP CHILD-ABUSE ASSOCIATION AND THE CHILDREN'S RETREAT CENTER. YOU CAN ENJOY MOUTH-WATERING MUFFINS...AND KNOW YOU'RE DOING GOOD FOR VICTIMS WHO CAN'T HELP THEMSELVES. MUFFINS-MEAN-HUGS–ALL THIS WEEK AT MOM'S MUFFINS.

PRESS KIT CHECKLIST

Think about your promotional goals and what you could include in a press kit. Write your notes here.

PRESS RELEASE TOPIC:

COVER LETTER FROM? (WHO):

INCLUDE A FACT SHEET?   Yes _____   No _____

INCLUDE PSAS?   Yes _____   No _____

INCLUDE A CLIENT LIST?   Yes _____   No _____
(If yes, answer the following question)

    Are all permissions obtained from clients?

    (Name of Client)   Yes _____   No _____

    _____   Yes _____   No _____

    _____   Yes _____   No _____

If the following items are included in the press kit, fill in the blanks.

BIO(S) OF:

PHOTO(S) (WHO/WHAT):

CLIPS (ALL, OR WHICH ONES):

REFERRAL LETTERS (ALL, OR WHICH ONES):

PRE-WRITTEN INTERVIEW FEATURING:

SAMPLE QUESTIONS ABOUT:

GETTING MAGAZINE PLACEMENTS

To get magazines to write about your organization, approach them in the same manner as newspapers—with a press release or press kit. Remember that a media advisory is less effective with magazines than with newspapers. Magazines often work months ahead of schedule. It is unlikely they will write about a scheduled event unless it is of great interest to them.

A better way to get your name in magazines is to offer yourself as a source for information. If your community has a free-lance writer's group, find the name of the contact person and inquire about a list of members. Perhaps you'll want to speak to selected writers about your organization. If you have special knowledge or an attractive communication style, there's a good chance you will be interviewed by a free-lance writer or a magazine writer.

Free-lance writers can be powerful allies. Established writers in your area might write for top magazines. Keep in mind, however, that writers are *reporters*–not publicists. Provide them with information when requested. Don't ask them to slant the story in your favor, give you extensive quotes, or not interview a competitor. Do not offer to pay them. They will be paid by the magazine.

You also might hire a free-lance writer with publicity skills. Remember that you are hiring the writer as a publicist. If the writer also accepts payment from a magazine while being paid by you to place the story, the writer has committed a breach of ethics and you should withdraw from working with that writer.

When hiring a writer, keep in mind that you are paying for that person's talent and skills. While you should provide general direction, allow the writer to contribute his or her ideas and help shape your project. You'll benefit from the writer's talent.

MEDIA FOLLOW-UP CALLS

Once you have sent materials to the media, your job is only half-finished. A follow-up call is crucial to the success of a publicity campaign.

In some public relations agencies, newcomers get the "dread task" of making follow-up calls to the media. In other agencies, experienced professionals make the calls, since the placement might be of utmost importance to the client.

There are many producers and editors who are bombarded with information. Many times a brusque, "just send in the information," is the norm. Don't get boxed in by your emotions. View follow-up calls as work getting done. Do your best and proceed on even keel. Allow yourself a minute of misery after a rough conversation, then forget it and move ahead.

Rehearse your presentation before making the calls. Know the details so thoroughly that you do not have to read a script or fumble through papers while you are talking to the media. The best approach is to be concise, relaxed and interesting.

Do not pour out as much information as possible on the phone. Some successful people make it a practice to limit this information to two minutes. If you go on longer, it is likely that the person isn't listening, but doodling instead.

Involve the other person in your idea. If you sense a positive response, let your enthusiasm show and ask a question that invites a response. If you hear a lukewarm response, lower your excitement level to a more businesslike tone. Gauging appropriate "levels" takes time, but it works. Often, a disinterested editor re-thinks an idea if the caller persists evenly (without hype). However, if this same editor, not having a good day, hears a voice that is more and more pumped up, he or she will turn off and reject the idea.

Do not open your call with, "Did you get my information?" Instead say "I recently sent you the information on _____, and would like to provide some additional information. Do you have a minute?"

FOLLOW-UP CALL—
THE RIGHT WAY

Following is an example of a good follow-up call:

Publicist: Hello, Mr. Jones?

TV Producer: Yes?

Publicist: I'm John Abbott, calling about Jevon Berk, the national champion ice skater who will make a special appearance at the WinterSports Shop at Hamilton Mall.

TV Producer: Uh Huh! I think I saw your release.

Publicist: Ms. Berk will arrive in town next week and I was wondering if you might have an opening for an interview on the 'Peter Cain Show.'

TV Producer: We're booked up. We just had an ice skater on last month—Maxine Jarvis. She's an Olympic medalist, too.

Publicist: I saw the show. It was excellent. Jevon Berk is different, though. She's the only ice skater who is also a magician. Believe it or not, she performs magic tricks while she's skating!

TV Producer: You're kidding.

Publicist: Nope. In fact, we have footage of her doing a spectacular trick during her last show.

TV Producer: Can you provide us with that footage?

Publicist: Certainly.

TV Producer: When will she be in town?

Publicist: She'll be here Monday through Thursday.

TV Producer: All right. Send me the footage. If it's good. I'll see if I can move our interview with a financial advisor scheduled for Tuesday. Call me back Thursday and I'll let you know.

Publicist: All right, I will.

FOLLOW-UP CALL—
THE WRONG WAY

This example is a poor way to follow-up. Can you explain why the example on page 53 is superior to this approach?

Publicist: Mr. Jones?

TV Producer: Yes?

Publicist: Hi! I'm John Abbott, the publicist for Jevon Berk. Did you get my information in the mail?

TV Producer: Uh huh, I think I saw your release.

Publicist: Ms. Berk is a skater/magician who's knocking the socks off of audiences from New Jersey to New Caledonia. She's the star of the magnificent show, 'World of Ice,' and you'd love her for the 'Peter Cain Show.' She's about five-foot-five, with long, black hair, and she's very telegenic. She can tell stories about...

TV Producer: Wait a minute, wait a minute! We just had an ice skater on the show.

Publicist: But Ms. Berk is *different*! She does magic tricks while she ice skates—juggling, card tricks, handkerchiefs—the whole kit and kaboodle! She'll raise your ratings, I guarantee that. She was a big hit on the 'Wally Walters Show' in Baltimore—they gave her a whole 14 minutes on the show, and she—

TV Producer: We got your material, we'll take a look at it.

Publicist: 'Take a look'? I can't urge you strongly enough to book her for the show! Don't you see what a terrific guest she'd be? You could—

TV Producer: I said, we'll see!

Publicist: Why don't I have Ms. Berk call you directly? Then you could—

TV Producer: No! (Hangs up).

FOLLOW-UP PHONE CALL TIPS

1. You should address your material to the appropriate editor or producer. Ask for that person on the phone. If a receptionist or secretary tells you the editor or producer isn't in, don't leave a message. Ask for the best time to reach that person, and call back later.

   You may have to call several times to reach your contact. This is better than leaving messages, because: (a) you're asking a lot of the editor or producer to call you back when that person doesn't know you; and (b) if you have to leave more than one message, you might be considered a nuisance before you have time to pitch your idea.

2. If an editor or producer says, "You'll need to talk with the assignment editor first," believe it. Ask for that editor's name; ask whether you should send new material. It's likely that the material will be sent inter-office to the assignment editor. Wait a few days, if there is no stringent time limit on your program, and call the assignment editor.

3. If an associate producer says, "I handle all his bookings. Maybe you can tell me about the idea," go ahead and discuss it. This is how many editors/producers operate.

4. If you have difficulty getting through on the phone, send a follow-up letter, asking a producer or editor to call you. If you don't hear back, try again on the phone.

5. If you must talk with an assignment editor who says, "You don't need to call—we consider every idea that comes in," approach him/her next time with, "I called to provide some fresh information on _____." Give yourself an excuse to call back as often as it makes sense.

6. Don't hound the media with follow-up calls. Your initial phone call should reach a conclusion: (a) yes; (b) no; (c) we'll consider it; (d) we may do a story later. Only (c) and (d) merit further calling. It is best—if the media approach is not timely or tied to a specific event—to send a new release or new letter a few weeks later. This can give the idea a new life and result in the interview or story placement.

PART THREE

THE OUTCOME

YOU'VE GOT AN INTERVIEW!

You've done it. You have an interview on a TV show; or you have a radio talk-show appearance; or you will be interviewed by the newspaper or magazine.

In a sense, much of your work is done. The interview won't be a cinch, but the plan calls for framing your story proposition to get a positive outcome. Once a producer, editor, or reporter has shown enough interest to schedule an interview with you, your idea has been endorsed.

Still, care must be taken to make the interview go smoothly. Following are tips for interviews with various media.

PRINT INTERVIEW TIPS

- If a reporter calls you for an interview you did not initiate, determine why he/she is calling. Ask for the deadline and say that you will call back well before the deadline.

- If you feel unprepared and uncertain, do not let the reporter interview at that time. Ask if you can schedule it at a later time.

- Don't let a reporter tour your business or facility unless everything is in top shape and the staff is prepared. It is very difficult to change a first impression.

- Interviewees who are unskilled in diplomacy or insecure will benefit from rehearsal. Practice so that the kinks are ironed out before the real interview.

- Avoid jargon and acronyms.

RADIO INTERVIEW TIPS

- Don't be fooled in thinking that how you dress isn't important, since no one can see you on radio. Dressing sharply can shape your attitude and give you a professional confidence.

- Use the minutes before the interview to stretch and warm up your voice. A brief conversation and a few deep breaths will help prep your voice for radio.

- Most radio shows have breaks for commercials or announcements. Use that time to relax and to clear your throat. (Your host may wish to do some prepping for the next segment by discussing briefly with you subjects that will be covered.)

- If you are on a show with call-ins, be careful never to become defensive. A good host will defuse hostile harangues. Do your best to answer questions in a positive and friendly manner. If stuck, feel free to say, "I'm sorry, I'm not the best person to answer that question," or simply "I don't know" when you are unsure.

| TIP FOR ANY INTERVIEW: |

When a reporter asks if a comment can be made "off the record," be careful. Some reporters respect "off the record" comments, but others do not.

TV APPEARANCE TIPS

If you have a television interview appearance, following are some tips.

- Men should wear a conservative tailored dark suit with a blue shirt. Women have more flexibility but should not stray far from basic colors and styles. Avoid wearing white or clothing with a fine print/design. White can reflect and a design will waver.

- Relax. Avoid nervous gestures or mannerisms. Take a few deep breaths before the camera is on.

- If you wear tinted glasses, remove them for the interview. Viewers want to see your eyes.

- A minute before you're on air, use a small pocket mirror to check hair, face, and overall appearance.

- Sit erect but not stiff. If your chair is uncomfortable, find a good position before going on the air. Relax, but don't slump.

- If the interview begins to get argumentative or negative, keep your voice calm and look relaxed.

- If a subject comes up that you aren't prepared to discuss, say so. It is better to avoid a topic than try to fake an answer.

- Following the interview, a director may want to shoot extra footage without sound (for intros or credits). Keep your movements consistent with those of the interview. Remember that you're still on camera and act accordingly.

- Do not speak loudly. The microphone will be adjusted to your voice level. Speak in a natural, audible tone.

- If possible, rehearse the interview several times with an associate.

- Remember that TV moves at a quicker pace. Keep your answers brief and to the point. Don't try to override the host when he/she says it's time for a commercial break or another guest.

GETTING MORE MILEAGE FROM YOUR COVERAGE THROUGH CLIPS

Gaining a publicity placement has dual benefits. First, is the increased visibility you receive when you appear on TV or radio, or have an article published in a newspaper or magazine.

There is more. You can also use your previous accomplishments to gain credibility, leverage, or stature, in the form of "clips."

These stories/appearances are excellent for marketing your product or service.

Obtaining "Clips"

If you notify a TV or radio station before your interview that you'd like a copy of your appearance, they will make the necessary arrangements. Some TV stations charge a fee for this service, but normally it is reasonable.

Many stations will simply ask you to bring a blank audio/videocassette and they will provide a copy of your appearance by the time you leave. Don't wait till weeks after your appearance or you might never get a copy of the tape.

Don't ask a reporter or editor at a newspaper or magazine to send you a copy of an article when it is published. This is a frequent request but not often honored. Newspaper and magazine writers don't have time. You can find the publication and do it yourself. If the interview was with an out-of-town periodical, ask the publication date—and either visit a large bookstore or newsstand that sells out-of-town journals, or write for a copy at the publication's source.

WAYS TO USE CLIPS

WAYS TO USE BROADCAST CLIPS

1. As a promotion piece to reinforce your credibility.

2. As something to show to employees (or potential employees).

3. As something to show or play for clients for sales purposes; or if a nonprofit group, to volunteers or donors.

WAYS TO USE PRINT CLIPS

Previously published articles about your organization can be useful in many ways, including:

1. Extracting good quotes, for brochure or sales promotion use. (Make sure you receive proper permission before circulating your promotional piece.)

2. Sending along with a direct mail letter to reinforce your position.

3. Sharing with employees (or perspective employees) to educate them about the organization.

4. Sending to other periodicals, along with a cover letter, to suggest a similar article or story.

CRISIS PUBLIC RELATIONS

Accidents will happen. A product goes awry. A building collapses. A key employee is arrested.

If you are destined to handle a major crisis, do your best to get help from a public relations agency that is experienced at handling this type of situation. For a smaller crisis, the following are a few basic suggestions:

1. Decide beforehand who will be the spokesperson for your organization. Select a person who can think and speak clearly during a confusing time.

2. Try not to use the phrase, "No comment." It often sounds guilty. Instead say, "I can't comment until I learn the facts" or, "It's not appropriate for me to comment on proprietary information" or, "For reasons of personal privacy, I cannot comment."

3. Tell what you know. Be as honest as possible without harming your organization. Don't lie. Give accurate information as soon as possible to fight rumors.

4. If there are injuries do not release names; the hospital will do that.

5. Don't speculate on the cause of an event. Also, do not speculate on monetary amounts (cost of damage, replacement value, or settlements of any kind).

SPECIAL EVENTS

Sometimes, a special event that creates publicity is a good idea:

- A local market sponsors free cooking lessons;

- A bicycle manufacturer schedules a city-wide "fun ride" to benefit a charity;

- A new company president is honored at a widely attended wine-and-cheese reception.

A word of warning: special events are not for the weak-willed. They must be coordinated by someone who plans well. To be successful, the responsible person should be organized and like detail work. Special events can be costly so a budget is required. Also, most events should have a primary purpose other than gaining media attention (as seen thoughout this book, there are less expensive ways to get such attention).

Special events can also be subject to the whims of nature. A heavy rain can ruin an outdoor event. Or you might discover that your event is scheduled the same day as "the big game". Or, the person delivering the cake has a car accident and never shows up. Anything can happen.

Negativity aside, there are things you can do to make your event go smoothly. Following are some suggestions:

HOLDING AN EVENT: A CHECKLIST

☑ 1. Plan the type of event. (The cost range listed below obviously depends on how you enhance the event with food, entertainment, and the number of guests).

Expensive	Meal (breakfast, brunch, luncheon, dinner)
	Live Entertainment event
	Social Hour (with hors d'oeuvres and drinks*)
	Conference
	Evening event (dance, party)
Moderately Expensive	Wine-and-cheese reception
	Seminar/Workshop
	Exhibit
Modest	Ceremony
	Tour of Facility
	Tea/Coffee

*Keep in mind that serving alcoholic beverages can put you in a position of liability. It is a good idea to maintain moderation in this situation.

☑ 2. Plan the details and create a budget. Following are some basic factors to consider:
- Appropriate meeting space (size, quality)
- Food/catering (type, amount)
- Hotel/guest accommodations (if required)
- Signage, banners, posters (type, number)
- Nametags, workbooks, flyers (type, number)
- Invitations and postage (quality, timing)
- Flowers/decorating (amount, type)
- Audiovisual equipment (type)
- Speakers' honorariums; awards, prizes
- Electricians, carpenters (if required)
- Chair and table rentals, etc.
- Publicity (amount, type)

EVENT CHECKLIST (continued)

Meeting space is often difficult to figure, but following is a rough guideline:

5-15 persons:	400 square feet
15-50 persons:	800 square feet
50-100 persons:	1,200 square feet
100-200 persons:	2,000 square feet
200-400 persons:	2,000-4,000 square feet

If you're renting space, the hotel/meeting space representative should be able to estimate the space required for your event.

Food/catering takes careful planning and consideration. If you're using a hotel meeting room, you often can get the space at no charge if you use their food service. Paying for space and hiring your own catering service can be more expensive or less expensive depending on your wants and needs. Check several options.

If you hire a caterer, check references before signing any agreements. Also, call the week and day before the event to make sure everything is going smoothly. It is often better to spend extra money and go with a quality caterer. Your event can be spoiled if the caterer does a poor job, or worse, doesn't show up.

3. Develop publicity angles for the event and notify appropriate media for coverage.

- Theme, slogan, speakers, location, guests—are they newsworthy?
- Timing; will it conflict with other events (election, holiday, graduation, etc.)?
- Can the event be co-sponsored by a newsworthy organization, or can it benefit a charity?

EVENT CHECKLIST (continued)

☑ 4. Create a timetable. General guidelines:

LONG RANGE

- Determine type of event, audience, and whether speakers will be needed (if so, attempt to book them early). Determine date of event. Do all the budget, timetable, and publicity planning.

TIP: Call the local Chamber of Commerce for the date you've selected to ensure there are no conflicting events scheduled.

- Decide how to invite (invitations? flyers? posters? other?).
- Select and confirm location.
- Develop format or outline of program.
- Select food/catering arrangements.

MID RANGE

- Have printed materials designed.
- Select menu.
- Plan publicity.
- Mail invitations (with response card—remember that paying return. postage will give you a more accurate RSVP rate).
- Plan audio-visual needs and room requirements (chairs, tables, etc.).

SHORT RANGE

- Confirm catering, speakers, program content, and other details; assess RSVPs.

ONE WEEK AHEAD

- Re-check and confirm all details.

TIP: Involve other people in planning your special event. They will develop ideas you didn't think of (no matter how creative you are) and can help in last-minute panics.

SUMMARY

You've now seen what it takes to get a story placed, create a press kit, bring an idea to the television screen and/or elevate your organization to a higher level of recognition or status. You have learned to assert a product or service so that people will know and talk about it.

By gaining an understanding of publicity, you have begun to develop a powerful tool. This book has provided an assessment of the various methods of publicity and helped you select the best for your particular need.

When publicity efforts are properly made, there is always a feeling of success. Even if you do not achieve your desired goal, you will earn the respect of important editors, reporters, producers, and other media personnel. This should make it easier for you the next time around.

Publicity is a prime part of marketing or advertising. It is also more. It is that good feeling when your business profits because of good publicity; or when your organization's cause makes a positive impact on the community. That is when publicity power is at it's best.

SUGGESTED READING:

1. *Effective Public Relations* by Scott M. Cutlip, et al. 640 pages, Prentice-Hall, 1985.
2. *Getting Publicity* by David M. Rees. 96 pages, David & Charles, 1984.
3. *How to Advertise and Promote Your Small Business* by Connie McClung Siegel. 128 pages, John Wiley & Sons, Inc., 1978.
4. *How to Handle Your Own Public Relations* by H. Gordon Lewis. 251 pages, Nelson-Hall, 1976.
5. *How to Promote Your Own Business* by Gary Blake and Robert W. Bly. New American Library, 1983.
6. *How to Publicize Your Way to Success* by Bonnie Weiss. Catalyst Publications, 1985.
7. *Media Marketing: How to Get Your Name and Story in Print and On the Air* by Peter G. Miller. 224 pages. Harper & Row, 1987.
8. *Practical Handbook of Public Relations* by Robert S. Cole. Prentice-Hall, 1981.
9. *Practical Publicity: How to Boost Any Cause* by David Tedone. 176 pages, Harvard Common Press, 1983.
10. *Professional's Guide to Publicity* by Richard Weiner. 176 pages, Public Relations, 1982.
11. *Promotions: Products, Services, Ideas* by William A. Kincaid. 416 pages, Merrill, 1985.
12. *Public Relations and Promotion Handbook: A Complete Guide for Small Business* by Linda Carlson. 272 pages, Van Nos Reinhold, 1982.
13. *Public Relations for the Entrepreneur and the Growing Business* by Norman R. Sodenberg. Probus Publishing, 1986.
14. *A Publicity and Public Relations Guide for Business* by Bruce A. Brough. 200 pages, Successful Business Library, 1984.
15. *Publicity and Public Relations Workbook* by Raymond Simon. 340 pages, Macmillan, 1983.
16. *Publicity for Books and Authors* by Peggy Glenn. 180 pages, Aames-Allen, 1985.
17. *Publicity: How to Get It* by Richard O'Brien. 176 pages, Harper & Row, 1977.
18. *Public Relations: How to Make the Media Work for You* by Ted Klein and Fred Danzig. 304 pages, Scribner's, 1985.
19. *The Publicity Manual* by Kate Kelly. 184 pages, Visibility ent., 1980.
20. *Tooting Your Own Horn: The Retailer's Guide to Public Relations.* National Retail Merchants.
21. *The Unabashed Self-Promoters Guide* by Dr. Jeffrey Lant. 366 pages, Jeffrey Lant Associates, 1983.

NOTE: All personal names (except for that of the author), business names, street addresses, telephone numbers, and information given in the sample releases and letters in this book are fictitious. Any similarity to actual persons, businesses, or events is unintentional.

ABOUT THE AUTHOR

Charles Mallory is a publicist who has seen his efforts result in stories and interviews in *The Wall Street Journal*, Cable News Network, in newspapers and national magazines in the U.S. and Great Britain, and on TV and radio shows in major U.S. cities.

Mallory has been a newspaper phototgrapher/reporter, magazine editor and radio station copywriter. He spent his early career in publicity working for Fleishman-Hillard, Inc., an international public relations firm. More recently, Mallory has worked as a publicist for Fred Pryor, and other leading motivational speakers.

He has been involved at every level of publicity programs, ranging from mega-campaigns (involving media coverage to millions of people) to small efforts that had a budget of less than $250.

Mallory operates a public relations and free-lance writing firm, Mallory Communications. He welcomes readers' comments. Please write to: Mallory Communications, P.O. Box 22403, Kansas City, MO 64113-2403.

NOTES

NOTES

OVER 150 BOOKS AND 35 VIDEOS AVAILABLE IN THE 50-MINUTE SERIES

We hope you enjoyed this book. If so, we have good news for you. This title is part of the best-selling *50-MINUTE*™ *Series* of books. All *Series* books are similar in size and identical in price. Many are supported with training videos.

To order *50-MINUTE* Books and Videos or request a free catalog, contact your local distributor or Crisp Publications, Inc., 1200 Hamilton Court, Menlo Park, CA 94025. Our toll-free number is (800) 442-7477.

50-Minute Series Books and Videos Subject Areas...

Management
Training
Human Resources
Customer Service and Sales Training
Communications
Small Business and Financial Planning
Creativity
Personal Development
Wellness
Adult Literacy and Learning
Career, Retirement and Life Planning

Other titles available from Crisp Publications in these categories

Crisp Computer Series
The Crisp Small Business & Entrepreneurship Series
Quick Read Series
Management
Personal Development
Retirement Planning